Train Your Brain to Stop Overthinking

Johann Horsley

30 Strategies to Fight Procrastination, Enhance Productivity and Focus on the Present

Contents

INTRODUCTION 7

Understanding Overthinking 7

Defining Overthinking and Its Impact................................. 7

The Connection Between Overthinking and Procrastination.................. 9

The Toll on Productivity and Mental Well-being...................... 10

CHAPTER 1 13

Setting Clear Goals 13

The Importance of Goal Setting 13

SMART Goals and How to Apply Them 14

Breaking Down Goals into Manageable Tasks 16

CHAPTER 2 19

Overcoming Perfectionism 19

Identifying Perfectionistic Tendencies 19

Embracing Imperfection 20

Learning from Mistakes 21

CHAPTER 3 23

Time Management Techniques 23

The Pomodoro Technique 23

Time Blocking Strategies 24

Prioritizing Tasks for Maximum Impact............................... 25

CHAPTER 4 27

Cultivating a Positive Mindset... 27

The Influence of Positive Thinking 27

Overcoming Negative Thought Patterns.............................. 28

Affirmations and Visualization Techniques 29

CHAPTER 5 31

Decluttering Your Mind and Space...31

Clearing Mental Clutter 31

Organizing Your Physical Space 32

Minimalism for Mental Clarity 33

CHAPTER 6 35

Creating Healthy Habits..35

The Science of Habit Formation 35

Breaking Bad Habits 36

Establishing Routines for Success...37

CHAPTER 7 39

The Art of Decision-Making..39

Overcoming Decision Paralysis...39

Strategies for Making Informed Decisions 40

Trusting Your Intuition 41

CHAPTER 8 43

Balancing Work and Life...43

Avoiding Burnout..43

Setting Boundaries 44

Finding Leisure in the Present Moment 45

CHAPTER 9 47

Embracing Change..47

Understanding the Nature of Change 47

Adapting to Unexpected Challenges 48

Using Change as a Catalyst for Growth 49

CHAPTER 10 51

Developing Resilience.. 51

Building Mental Resilience 51

Coping with Setbacks 52

Turning Challenges into Opportunities 53

CHAPTER 11 55

Connecting with Others... 55

The Importance of Social Support..................................... 55

Effective Communication Skills 56

Collaborative Problem-Solving 57

CHAPTER 12 59

Mastering the Art of Focus.. 59

Techniques for Improving Concentration 59

Minimizing Distractions... 60

Training Your Brain to Stay Present................................... 61

CHAPTER 13 63

Mind-Body Connection.. 63

Incorporating Physical Activity for Mental Clarity............. 63

Mindful Eating and its Impact 64

The Role of Sleep in Overcoming Overthinking.................. 65

CHAPTER 14 67

Nurturing Creativity.. 67

Unleashing Your Creative Potential................................... 67

Embracing Divergent Thinking 68

Using Creativity to Solve Problems 69

CHAPTER 15 71

A Mindful and Productive Future 71

Reflecting on the Journey 71

Sustaining Positive Changes 72

Moving Forward with Confidence 73

INTRODUCTION

Understanding Overthinking

Overthinking has become an all too typical difficulty in our fast-paced environment, where information flows continuously and demands for our attention appear endless. By exploring the complexities of overthinking, its significant effects on our lives, and the frequently overlooked link between procrastination and overthinking and the consequences it has for our productivity and mental health, this chapter lays the groundwork for the rest of our trip.

Defining Overthinking and Its Impact

Fundamentally, overthinking is the act of continuously and frequently obsessively reflecting on ideas, possibilities, or choices. It goes beyond the typical thought processes we use to solve issues or make decisions. Overanalyzing turns into an endless cycle, a mental treadmill that impedes development and messes with the way ideas naturally flow.

Imagine a mind imprisoned in a labyrinth of its own making, where each and every choice—no matter how insignificant—is examined and evaluated from every conceivable perspective. In addition to depleting mental energy, this perpetual analysis paralysis causes indecision and a feeling of overwhelm.

Overanalyzing can take many different forms, such reliving the past, fretting about the future, or conjuring up hypothetical situations that might never happen. Overthinking has negative effects on emotional stability, physical health, and general quality of life in addition to its mental effects.

It's critical to acknowledge the variety of overthinking's expressions as we go deeper into its complexities. Some people might be caught in a never-ending loop of self-doubt, while others might find themselves dwelling on previous transgressions. The first step to escaping the clutches of overthinking is to recognize these patterns.

The Connection Between Overthinking and Procrastination

Although procrastination and overthinking may appear to be separate problems, they are actually intimately related and frequently feed off one another in a vicious cycle. The act of putting off chores or decisions, or procrastination, is frequently motivated by the need for perfection or the fear of making the incorrect option. This worry then sets off a vicious cycle of overthinking that impedes advancement.

Imagine a situation where a project deadline is approaching quickly. An excessive amount of time may be spent by the overthinker analyzing different strategies, imagining potential hazards, and second-guessing every choice. Consequently, the person becomes ensnared in the procrastination trap and delays the actual task.

It is essential to comprehend this relationship in order to end the cycle. People can overcome the constraints of procrastination and make more timely and efficient decisions by addressing the underlying reasons of overthinking.

The Toll on Productivity and Mental Well-being

Overanalyzing has consequences that go far beyond incomplete work and missed deadlines. It has a significant negative psychological and emotional impact on one's general well-being and productivity. Overthinking's emotional burden and incessant mental chatter can cause tension, worry, and even burnout.

Overthinkers may become mired in a perfectionist cycle at work, wherein innovation and creativity are stifled by a fear of making mistakes. Time and energy wasted on pointless contemplation instead of taking action reduces productivity. Reaching one's full potential is impeded by overthinking.

Overanalyzing can cause stress and uncertainty in relationships because it is a constant source of worry and indecision. It could result in lost chances since trying new things or pursuing objectives can become extremely difficult due to fear of rejection or failure.

The impact on mental health is especially noticeable. Overanalyzing can be a part of a negative thought pattern that lowers self-worth and fuels feelings of inadequacy. Self-critical thoughts collide with the need for assurance and confidence, creating a mental battlefield.

The first step to liberty is realizing how overthinking affects productivity and mental health. In the ensuing chapters, we will delve into doable tactics for releasing oneself from the shackles of overanalyzing and cultivating a more aware and fruitful way of being. By means of comprehension, consciousness, and deliberate behavior, we can rewire our minds to surmount excessive contemplation and welcome a more satisfying and harmonious living.

12

CHAPTER 1

Setting Clear Goals

Having definite, attainable goals is a fundamental step in the process of teaching our minds to cease overanalyzing. As a feeling of direction and guidance through the difficulties of life, goals act as lighthouses. This chapter delves into the significance of goal formation, presents the SMART criteria for successful goal creation, and helps readers break down more ambitious goals into smaller, more doable tasks.

The Importance of Goal Setting

Setting goals helps us translate our desires from intangible visions into tangible deeds. Having specific goals helps people focus their efforts more effectively, both personally and professionally. Without objectives, the mind has no clear aim to focus on, which makes it more likely to give in to overthinking.

Think of it as a ship traversing a huge ocean. The ship would float aimlessly without a destination, at the mercy of the winds and currents. In a similar vein, those who lack specific goals could end themselves lost in a sea of overanalyzing and always doubting their direction and purpose.

Establishing goals helps to spark motivation. The path takes on greater meaning and satisfaction when we have a clear idea of what we want to accomplish. As milestones are met, goals give a sense of accomplishment that boosts confidence and chases away the clouds of uncertainty that sometimes accompany overthinking.

SMART Goals and How to Apply Them

A structured framework for goal-setting is provided by the SMART goal idea, which guarantees that targets are time-bound, relevant, measurable, and specified. This process converts abstract goals into concrete, doable objectives, which serves as a potent counterbalance to overanalyzing.

Specific: Clearly state your goals for yourself. Having clear objectives helps to reduce the uncertainty that encourages overthinking by giving focus and clarity. For instance, a specific aim might be to "run a 5K in under 30 minutes," as opposed to a general one like "improve fitness."

Measurable: Set standards for gauging advancement. Measurable objectives provide a feeling of success by enabling monitoring and assessment. An example of a measurable objective, using the fitness example, might be "lose 10 pounds in two months."

Achievable: Make sure your objectives are both reasonable and doable. Although having ambition is admirable, having unrealistic expectations can cause dissatisfaction and overthinking as a result. Make sure your objectives are in line with your resources and capabilities.

Relevant: Make sure your objectives have purpose and are in line with your overarching goals. Relevant goals are more likely to be dropped, which adds to a feeling of aimlessness that encourages overanalyzing.

Time-Bound: Set a deadline for accomplishing your objectives. Time-bound objectives instill a sense of urgency and ward off procrastination, which is a frequent side effect of overanalyzing. For example, "complete a professional certification in six months."

By incorporating the SMART criteria into your goal-setting process, you can turn vague aspirations into workable strategies and provide yourself a methodical strategy that helps reduce the ambiguity and indecision that come with overanalyzing.

Breaking Down Goals into Manageable Tasks

Setting big, broad goals is vital, but so is breaking them down into smaller, more doable tasks. Big objectives can be intimidating, which makes the mind overthink the situation as it tries to process how big the work is.

Setting goals in smaller steps does two crucial things: it gives the journey a more manageable scope and a progress roadmap. People can concentrate on doing little tasks and gaining momentum and confidence gradually rather than obsessing about the final outcome.

When writing a book, for instance, one could have a broad goal like "finish a 300-page manuscript." Upon breaking this down, smaller goals could be like "write 1,000 words per day," "outline chapters," or "conduct research for specific sections." All of these are doable and help towards the overall objective.

This chapter acknowledges that progress is made little by little and invites readers to embrace the art of goal-breaking. By doing this, the daunting aspect of big goals is lessened, which lessens the propensity to overthink things through and gives one a feeling of control over their path.

As we continue to investigate how to teach the brain to stop overanalyzing, setting specific goals becomes an essential tactic. People can reduce their tendency to overthink things by using SMART goal planning and the technique of breaking down large goals into smaller, more achievable tasks. This gives them a roadmap that will help them live a more meaningful and purposeful life.

CHAPTER 2

Overcoming Perfectionism

Perfectionism is a powerful enemy that frequently surfaced in our quest to teach our minds to cease overthinking. This chapter explores the complex mechanics of perfectionism, helping readers recognize their own perfectionistic inclinations, accept imperfection, and gain insightful knowledge from the mistakes we will inevitably make along the way.

Identifying Perfectionistic Tendencies

Perfectionism is an obsession with flawlessness that can frequently result in paralysis rather than just the pursuit of perfection. The first step to breaking free from perfectionistic inclinations' hold on our ideas and behaviors is to recognize them. It can take many different forms, such having excessively high expectations, being afraid of criticism, or completely avoiding work out of fear of failing.

The mentality of a perfectionist is a harsh critic, examining every little detail and emphasizing any perceived shortcomings. Decisions become burdened with the weight of irrational expectations as a result of this hyperfocus on perfection. It is essential to recognize and understand these inclinations in order to break free from the overthinking loop and develop a more positive outlook.

Embracing Imperfection

Unlike what perfectionists think, imperfection is a necessary part of being human, not a sign of weakness. Accepting imperfection is a freeing experience that enables people to release themselves from the crippling need for perfection. It entails redefining inadequacies and failures as chances for improvement as opposed to proof of inferiority.

A common cause of perfectionism is the fear of being judged—by oneself or by others. When people accept their imperfections, they break free from the chains of unceasing assessment and censure. Moments of imperfection turn into stepping stones, each adding to the greater tapestry of growth on the personal and professional fronts.

Accepting imperfection is a realization of the intrinsic beauty in life's ups and downs rather than a support of mediocrity. It enables the development of resilience in the face of setbacks, the exploration of creativity, and the acceptance of vulnerability. This paradigm change allows people to approach things with a greater sense of freedom and releases them from the hold of overthinking.

Learning from Mistakes

Make mistakes, and you will develop from them. They are not failures. Reframing mistakes as opportunities for learning becomes a radical effort of self-compassion in a society that frequently stigmatizes blunders. Learning from mistakes requires a change of viewpoint, where failures are seen as essential information points on the path to mastery rather than as signs of incapacity.

Perfectionism frequently views errors as disastrous, which leads to excessive reflection and self-doubt. People that have a growth mindset understand that making mistakes is a necessary component of learning. Every mistake provides a learning opportunity, highlighting areas for development and imparting the information required for future achievement.

The chapter exhorts readers to adopt an attitude that sees failures as opportunities for improvement. It looks at ways to reinterpret failure, develop resilience, and draw valuable lessons from setbacks. By owning up to their faults, people not only weaken the grip of perfectionism but also give themselves the skills necessary to face obstacles head-on and persevere.

To sum up, conquering perfectionism entails recognizing one's perfectionistic inclinations, accepting imperfection, and growing from errors. Overanalyzing becomes less common as people break free from the crippling grasp of perfectionism, creating more room for a more resilient and empathetic response to life's obstacles.

CHAPTER 3

Time Management Techniques

A valuable friend in the fight to retrain our minds and escape the grip of overthinking is efficient time management. Three important time management strategies are covered in this chapter: Prioritizing Tasks for Maximum Impact, Time Blocking Strategies, and the Pomodoro Technique. By becoming proficient in these methods, people may take back control of their calendars, increase productivity, and lessen the mental chaos that frequently results from overanalyzing.

The Pomodoro Technique

Taking its name from the Italian word for "tomato," the Pomodoro Technique is a time management technique meant to increase productivity and focus. Work is broken up Into 25-mlnute perlods with this technique, with quick breaks in between. This pattern is called a "Pomodoro," and four Pomodoros are followed by a lengthier rest.

Because the Pomodoro Technique gives jobs a planned and manageable approach, it is especially useful in the fight against overthinking. Setting a time limit for work allows people to focus on a task without having to worry about making a huge, ongoing commitment. This targeted approach lessens the chance of getting sidetracked and lessens the possibility of overanalyzing how big a project is.

The method also acts as a reminder to take regular pauses, which keeps the mind fresh and helps avoid burnout. By using the Pomodoro Technique consistently, one can escape the loop of overthinking that might come with prolonged, unfocused labor by teaching the mind to welcome intense work moments.

Time Blocking Strategies

As a time management technique, time blocking entails setting aside specified time slots for various projects or pursuits. Time blocking, as opposed to standard to-do lists, sets aside certain times for particular tasks, resulting in a visual depiction of how time will be spent during the day.

This tactic, which gives each day a distinct structure and goal, is effective in preventing overthinking. People can prevent the mental exhaustion that results from continually dividing their attention between unrelated tasks by allocating specific time slots to different tasks. Time blocking reduces the mental strain that comes with making decisions because the timetable directs the activities of the day.

Time blocking also teaches people to estimate work completion times realistically. In addition to preventing overcommitment, which can result in stress and overthinking, it fosters a sense of accountability. People who intentionally manage their time feel more in control of their schedules and experience less anxiety associated with obsessing about impending deadlines and incomplete work.

Prioritizing Tasks for Maximum Impact

Setting priorities is essential to time management success and a vital tactic in the fight against overthinking. President Dwight D. Eisenhower is credited with creating the Eisenhower Matrix, a tool that divides jobs into four quadrants according to their significance and urgency. This matrix serves as a roadmap for setting priorities and concentrating effort on projects that support overarching objectives.

The matrix is divided into four sections:

1.Important and Urgent: Things that need to be done right now.

2.Important but not Urgent: Activities that support long-term objectives yet might not require immediate attention.

3.Urgent but not important: Tasks that need to be completed right away but won't have a big long-term impact.

4.Non-urgent and non-important tasks: those that fall into neither category.

Sorting jobs into categories helps people focus on the things that will help them achieve their goals and lessens the chance that they will overthink unimportant things. This tactic guarantees that efforts are focused on projects that will actually make a difference, generating a feeling of satisfaction and reducing the mental clutter brought on by unimportant worries.

In conclusion, escaping the chains of overthinking requires learning time management strategies like the Pomodoro Technique, Time Blocking, and Prioritization. Over time, these techniques provide people direction, structure, and a feeling of control, enabling them to live a fruitful and balanced life and seize every opportunity.

CHAPTER 4

Cultivating a Positive Mindset

The ability to think positively emerges as a transforming force in our quest to train our brains and escape the grip of overthinking. This chapter examines the power of positive thinking, methods for breaking bad thought patterns, and real-world applications of visualization and affirmation exercises. Adopting an optimistic outlook enables people to overcome mental hurdles caused by overthinking and face issues head-on.

The Influence of Positive Thinking

Positive thinking is an intentional and proactive way of analyzing and dealing with life's obstacles, not just a transient optimism. Positive thinking has an impact that goes beyond the instantaneous emotional reaction; it affects perceptions, choices, and even the results of different circumstances.

People who have an optimistic outlook on life are more inclined to view issues as solvable opportunities rather than insurmountable roadblocks when faced with hardship. This perspective change makes it much less likely to overthink things because the emphasis moves from problem-solving to problem-hugging.

Positivity has a significant impact on mental health. It functions as a protective barrier against tension, worry, and melancholy, fostering a mental atmosphere that discourages overanalyzing. Fostering thankfulness, developing perseverance in the face of adversity, and teaching the mind to perceive possibilities in obstacles are all part of cultivating a positive mentality.

Overcoming Negative Thought Patterns

A common behavior that leads to overthinking is negative thought patterns. These tendencies can appear as increased attention to possible hazards, catastrophic thinking, or self-doubt. It takes conscious effort to break these tendencies by reframing ideas and substituting positive viewpoints for pessimistic ones.

Cognitive restructuring, a therapeutic approach that entails recognizing and disputing unfavorable thoughts, is one useful tactic. Overthinking can be broken by challenging the veracity of unfavorable ideas and substituting them with more realistic and balanced explanations.

Another effective tool is mindfulness, which enables people to examine their ideas objectively. People can choose not to interact with negative thinking patterns by becoming more conscious of them, which gradually reduces their influence. Deep breathing exercises and other mindfulness techniques offer a mental reset that lessens the effects of overthinking.

Affirmations and Visualization Techniques

Positive words that support desired behaviors or attitudes are called affirmations. Affirmations have the capacity to transform mental patterns and engender a more upbeat, self-empowering mindset when used regularly. Positive expressions of self-worth, competence, and optimism are used in affirmations to counterbalance the negative self-talk that frequently accompanies overthinking.

Using visualization techniques, one can visualize desired results in their mind. People can build a mental framework that is less prone to overthinking, lower anxiety, and boost confidence by clearly visualizing success and happy experiences. By bringing ideas and behaviors into alignment with desired results, visualization helps people adopt an optimistic outlook and stop worrying about future setbacks.

A powerful synergy is created when affirmations and imagery are combined, strengthening positive attitudes and beliefs. By incorporating these methods into everyday life, especially in stressful or uncertain times, one can gradually alter one's cognitive processes and develop a resilient, upbeat mindset.

To sum up, developing an optimistic outlook is a crucial first step in teaching the brain to stop overanalyzing. When people consistently practice affirmations and visualization techniques, together with techniques for breaking through negative thought patterns, they can overcome obstacles with grace and optimism. The grasp of overthinking releases as the mind turns into a positive refuge, creating space for a more harmonious and satisfying mental landscape.

CHAPTER 5

Decluttering Your Mind and Space

One important tactic in the quest to teach our brains to quit overanalyzing is to clear our physical environment as well as our mental space. This chapter delves into the nuances of reducing mental clutter, simplifying our physical environment, and adopting minimalism as a means of improving mental clarity. By purposefully streamlining our thoughts and surroundings, we lay the groundwork for a calmer, more concentrated mind.

Clearing Mental Clutter

Over time, mental clutter builds up due to the continuous stream of thoughts, obligations, and information competing for our attention. It adds to the phenomena of overthinking since an overworked mind finds it difficult to prioritize important activities and sort through the clutter.

People must first identify and accept the causes of their mental overload in order to free their minds of mental clutter. This entails determining which obligations are superfluous, dealing with outstanding problems, and establishing limits on the steady stream of information coming in from different sources.

Journaling and other mindfulness exercises are effective methods for clearing the mind. People are able to witness and let go of the mental chatter that fuels overthinking when they set aside time for silence and introspection. Anchors such as focused attention and mindful breathing help the mind to relax and regain clarity.

This chapter will cover useful methods for clearing the mind, such as learning to say no, engaging in mindfulness exercises, and scheduling deliberate relaxation periods. People can lessen the cognitive load that leads to overthinking and develop a more resilient and focused mind by making mental space.

Organizing Your Physical Space

Our mental health is significantly impacted by the condition of our physical environment. An untidy and disorderly space can exacerbate the overthinking process by adding to emotions of turmoil and overwhelm. Putting the room in order is a concrete step in establishing a setting that encourages concentration and mental clarity.

This chapter's portion walks readers through doable methods for organizing and decluttering their living and workspaces. Methodologies like the KonMari approach, which prioritizes retaining only things that "spark joy," offer a methodical way to simplify physical areas.

Establishing areas with defined uses, including work, rest, and sleeping, helps to provide a feeling of structure and direction. The idea of deliberate design—where a space's arrangement and function match its intended use—is examined in this chapter. By applying these ideas, people can design surroundings that help them achieve their objectives and lessen the mental chatter that results from overanalyzing.

Minimalism for Mental Clarity

As a way of living, minimalism promotes deliberate simplification and the deliberate elimination of excess. Practicing minimalism involves streamlining relationships, responsibilities, and mental processes in addition to getting rid of material belongings. When it comes to getting rid of overthinking, minimalism is a great tool for fostering mental clarity.

The concepts of minimalism and how they relate to different facets of life will be examined by readers. This entails cutting daily routines down, making decisions more easily, and letting go of material attachments that could cause brain clutter.

People can change their emphasis from pursuing more to appreciating what really matters by adopting minimalism. This deliberate way of life lessens the need to overthink acquiring things or negotiating challenging and congested surroundings by fostering a sense of fulfillment and purpose.

In summary, deliberate and methodical attempts to streamline and simplify are necessary for the process of clearing the mind and environment. People make space for a more intentional, focused, and serene living by adopting minimalism, arranging their physical spaces, and getting rid of mental clutter. Overanalyzing loses its hold on one when both the internal and external settings become more simple. This leads to a life that is more harmonious and balanced.

CHAPTER 6

Creating Healthy Habits

Developing good habits is a key tactic in our effort to retrain the brain and conquer the obstacles caused by overthinking. This chapter delves into the science of habit formation, the art of changing unhealthy behaviors, and creating successful routines. By comprehending the workings of habits and consciously molding our actions, we can lay the groundwork for leading a more conscious and meaningful life.

The Science of Habit Formation

Our daily behaviors and reactions are automatically shaped by our habits, which are the unseen builders of our existence. For those who want to use habits to combat overthinking, it is essential to comprehend the science of habit formation.

The cue, routine, and reward loop is what makes up a habit. The routine is the actual action, the reward serves to reinforce the habit, and the cue initiates the behavior. Through the identification of these constituents, people are able to examine and evaluate current behaviors, recognizing the cues and rewards that sustain them.

The idea of habit stacking, in which newly formed habits are linked to preexisting ones, is explored in this chapter. By utilizing the neuronal pathways already present in the brain, this tactic facilitates the formation and upkeep of positive behaviors. People can purposefully create routines that prevent overthinking and advance mental health by deliberately modifying the cues and rewards connected to their habits.

Breaking Bad Habits

It takes self-awareness, dedication, and deliberate substitution to break bad behaviors. Numerous overthinking-related activities, like excessive rumination or avoidance tactics, can be harmful to one's mental well-being. This chapter's part walks readers through the process of recognizing, comprehending, and swapping out unhealthy habits with better ones.

The idea of habit substitution—where people intentionally switch out a bad habit for a good one—is introduced in this chapter. By taking a deliberate approach, the hole left by breaking a habit is avoided and is instead filled with an activity that promotes general well-being. Developing accountability structures, asking for help, and establishing clear aims are examples of practical tactics that are crucial in the fight against overthinking.

Establishing Routines for Success

Establishing routines reduces the mental strain that comes with making decisions all the time by providing structure and predictability. Setting up routines becomes essential for success while trying to overcome overthinking. This section examines the components of successful routines and how they support concentration and mental clarity.

The significance of morning and evening routines—which act as the day's bookends, establishing the tone for concentration and equilibrium—will become clear to readers. The chapter also emphasizes the importance of consistency in the development of habits, stressing the necessity of making small, durable adjustments to everyday routines.

Routines are created using the scientifically proven principles of habit formation, which guarantee that they will become deeply embedded in everyday life. People can reduce the cognitive load associated with overthinking and produce an atmosphere that supports achievement and well-being by purposefully forming habits within established routines.

To sum up, developing healthy behaviors is a game-changing tactic in the fight against overthinking. Through comprehending the science behind habit formation, kicking bad habits, and creating success routines, people can develop a way of life that promotes resilience, mental clarity, and purpose. Overthinking loses its hold on a person when they develop beneficial behaviors that become second nature, leading to a more purposeful and happy life.

CHAPTER 7

The Art of Decision-Making

In the tapestry of life, decisions form the intricate patterns that shape our journey. The ability to navigate this realm skillfully is an art – the art of decision-making. This chapter delves into the nuances of overcoming decision paralysis, crafting strategies for making informed decisions, and recognizing the invaluable role of intuition in the decision-making process.

Overcoming Decision Paralysis

Decision paralysis, often characterized by an overwhelming array of choices leading to indecision, is a common challenge in the modern world. The sheer volume of options, coupled with the fear of making the wrong choice, can paralyze Individuals and hinder progress.

This section explores the root causes of decision paralysis, such as perfectionism and fear of failure. Readers will gain insights into the psychological factors that contribute to indecision and learn practical strategies to overcome decision paralysis.

The chapter introduces the concept of prioritization, helping individuals focus on the most impactful decisions and break down complex choices into manageable steps. Techniques such as the pros and cons list, decision matrices, and setting clear criteria become valuable tools in overcoming decision paralysis and moving forward with confidence.

Strategies for Making Informed Decisions

Informed decisions are the product of careful consideration, research, and a deep understanding of the available options. This section guides readers through the strategies for making informed decisions, emphasizing the importance of gathering relevant information, considering potential outcomes, and evaluating risks.

The chapter explores the significance of setting clear goals and aligning decisions with long-term objectives. Readers will learn to identify biases that may cloud judgment and employ critical thinking skills to assess information objectively.

Practical exercises and case studies illustrate the application of decision-making strategies in various contexts, from personal choices to professional endeavors. By adopting a systematic approach to decision-making, individuals can enhance their ability to make informed and strategic choices that align with their values and aspirations.

Trusting Your Intuition

While data and analysis are essential components of decision-making, there is another equally valuable tool – intuition. This section explores the role of intuition in the decision-making process and highlights the importance of trusting one's instincts.

Readers will gain an understanding of the subtle signals that intuition provides, such as gut feelings, emotional responses, and a sense of alignment with one's values. The chapter encourages individuals to cultivate self-awareness and listen to their intuition as a valuable source of guidance.

The art of balancing rational analysis with intuitive insights is discussed, illustrating how the integration of both aspects can lead to well rounded decisions. Case studies and anecdotes showcase instances where intuition played a pivotal role in successful decision-making.

In conclusion, the art of decision-making involves a delicate dance between overcoming decision paralysis, employing strategies for informed choices, and trusting the inner compass of intuition. By mastering this art, individuals can navigate the complex landscape of decisions with confidence, clarity, and a deep sense of alignment with their true selves. As they embark on this journey, readers are invited to embrace the multifaceted nature of decision-making and cultivate the skills necessary to craft a path forward with purpose and conviction.

CHAPTER 8

Balancing Work and Life

Finding a good balance between work and life is crucial if we are to train our minds and overcome overthinking. This chapter explores the crucial elements of preserving this balance, including preventing burnout, establishing limits, and finding leisure time in the here and now. People can design a satisfying and sustainable lifestyle by intentionally balancing the demands of their personal and professional lives.

Avoiding Burnout

In today's fast-paced world, burnout—a state of physical and mental weariness brought on by ongoing working stress—is a common problem. Burnout is a fertile ground for overthinking because the demands of work can be mentally taxing and reduce coping skills.

This chapter's portion examines burnout symptoms and the value of early intervention. The development of reasonable goals, taking regular breaks, and using time management techniques are just a few of the useful techniques for preventing burnout that readers will discover. The chapter highlights the need of self-care in preventing burnout and stresses the necessity of getting enough sleep, eating a healthy diet, and exercising to maintain general wellbeing.

Setting Boundaries

Setting up solid, unambiguous limits is essential to preserving a healthy work-life balance. Without these limits, the pressures of the workplace can seep into personal life, leading to overthinking and making it difficult to completely enjoy leisure and relaxation.

In order to successfully and assertively articulate their limits, readers will examine the art of boundary-setting. Setting priorities for work, developing the ability to say no, and scheduling specific time for personal activities are all effective methods for establishing boundaries. People can clear their minds by drawing clear boundaries between their personal and professional lives. This helps to lessen the mental clutter that frequently results from overanalyzing.

Finding Leisure in the Present Moment

Leisure is a purposeful and revitalizing participation with activities that bring happiness and pleasure; it is not just the absence of labor. This chapter's portion explores the value of leisure time spent in the present and how it helps prevent overthinking.

The idea of mindfulness in leisure will be explored by readers, who will learn how to completely engage in the activity at hand without being distracted by thoughts of the past or the future. People are able to escape the loop of overanalyzing and appreciate the richness of the present by taking part in leisure activities with awareness.

The chapter recognizes that each person has different things that help them relax and have fun, thus it recommends exploring a variety of leisure activities. Finding leisure time in the present is essential to living a balanced and meaningful life, whether it be through reading, taking nature walks, engaging in creative endeavors, or socializing with others.

In conclusion, teaching the brain to stop overthinking requires striking a balance between work and life. People can design a sustainable and fulfilling lifestyle by managing their stress levels through self-care, drawing clear boundaries between their personal and professional lives, and finding leisure time to enjoy the present. When the balance is achieved, the mental clutter that results from overanalyzing disappears, making life more dynamic and meaningful.

CHAPTER 9

Embracing Change

Life is full of change, and one of the most important things we can do to stop overthinking is to learn to accept it. The nature of change, coping mechanisms for unforeseen obstacles, and the transformational potential of utilizing change as a catalyst for both professional and personal growth are all covered in this chapter. People can reduce the mental obstacles brought on by overthinking and increase resilience by developing a mentality that accepts and manages change.

Understanding the Nature of Change

A fundamental and unavoidable aspect of the human experience is change. Change is a force that influences our journey, whether it be in personal relationships, work pathways, or larger life circumstances. Recognizing the inevitable nature of change and the fact that resistance frequently results in increased stress and overanalyzing are essential components of understanding its nature.

This chapter's part on the psychology of change examines typical responses and the influence of attitude on adaptability. The stages of change—from early denial to final acceptance—and the function of mindfulness in easing these changes will become clearer to readers.

Individuals can lessen the mental resistance that frequently accompanies uncertainty by accepting change as a normal and necessary part of life. This promotes a more adaptable and flexible mindset.

Adapting to Unexpected Challenges

Because life is unpredictable, unforeseen difficulties will inevitably come up. Resilience is typified by the capacity to adjust to these difficulties and is a powerful remedy for overanalyzing. This section offers useful techniques for handling unanticipated events and preserving mental clarity in the face of uncertainty.

The significance of adaptability, problem-solving abilities, and keeping an optimistic outlook in the face of unforeseen difficulties will be discussed with readers. For readers who are experiencing their own unforeseen obstacles, case studies and real-life examples show how people have effectively adjusted to unforeseen situations, offering motivation and advice.

People can reframe the story of change from one of fear to one of personal development by reinterpreting unforeseen obstacles as chances for growth and learning.

Using Change as a Catalyst for Growth

When accepted and handled thoughtfully, change can be a potent driver of both professional and personal development. This chapter's part walks readers through the process of viewing change as a chance to grow, learn, and reevaluate their course in life.

The idea of a growth mindset—in which obstacles are seen as chances to push one's limits and learn new abilities—is examined in this chapter. Through this book, readers will discover and dispel limiting ideas that can prevent them from using change as a catalyst for personal development.

Readers are encouraged to visualize their ideal future and choose concrete measures toward realizing that vision through practical exercises and introspection prompts. Through proactive story shaping, people can effectively harness the transformative power of change, which can help to develop a feeling of purpose and lessen the mental weight associated with overthinking.

In summary, accepting change involves more than just enduring life's ups and downs; it also entails actively taking part in the process of development and evolution. People can develop a mindset that embraces change by comprehending the nature of change, adjusting to unforeseen obstacles, and utilizing change as a fuel for growth. The tendency to overthink things reduces along with anxiety and aversion to change, enabling a more resilient and powerful response to life's always shifting circumstances.

CHAPTER 10

Developing Resilience

The foundation of mental toughness is resilience, which is essential for overcoming overthinking and gracefully conquering obstacles in life. This chapter examines how mental resilience develops, coping mechanisms for failures, and the transformational potential of transforming obstacles into opportunities. Resilience is a strong foundation that people can build for a more empowered and balanced life.

Building Mental Resilience

Mental resilience is the capacity to overcome hardship, endure setbacks, and constructively respond to obstacles. This chapter's section explores the essential elements of developing mental resilience, such as self-awareness, self-regulation, and a growth mindset.

The idea of emotional intelligence and how it improves resilience will be discussed with readers. The chapter offers helpful activities and methods for enhancing emotional resilience, including strengthening one's support system, practicing mindfulness, and cognitive reframing.

People who have developed mental resilience are better equipped to withstand life's adversities and less likely to overthink things when things are tough.

Coping with Setbacks

Since setbacks are an unavoidable part of life, developing coping mechanisms is crucial to preserving mental health. This section walks readers through coping mechanisms for failures, highlighting the value of perspective-taking, self-compassion, and flexibility.

Readers confronting their own obstacles will find inspiration and insights from case studies and real-life examples that demonstrate how people have overcome obstacles. The chapter promotes taking a constructive stance toward failures, seeing them as chances for development and learning rather than insurmountable roadblocks.

People might lessen their propensity to overthink during trying times by learning good coping strategies and reinterpreting failures as brief diversion rather than as permanent obstacles.

Turning Challenges into Opportunities

Resilience is defined as the capacity to see opportunities in adversity. The transformational power of redefining adversity is examined in this section, which encourages readers to see obstacles as opportunities for both professional and personal development.

When faced with obstacles, readers will gain useful techniques for changing their perspective, such as recognizing learning opportunities, establishing reasonable goals, and making use of support networks. The chapter places a strong emphasis on the role that self-efficacy—the conviction that one can overcome obstacles—plays in enabling people to turn obstacles into opportunities.

People can alleviate the psychological strain of excessive analysis and cultivate an outlook that welcomes the possibility of constructive change by taking a proactive and positive stance towards obstacles.

To sum up, cultivating resilience is a life-changing process that entails strengthening one's mental toughness, learning how to handle failures, and seeing obstacles as chances for improvement. By developing resilience, people lay the groundwork for a life that is more resilient and powerful, clearing out the mental clutter that comes with overanalyzing and adopting an attitude that flourishes in the face of difficulty.

CHAPTER 11

Connecting with Others

The difficulties that arise from overthinking can be effectively countered by human interaction, which offers a source of assistance, comprehension, and cooperative problem-solving. In order to build meaningful connections with people, this chapter examines the significance of social support, effective communication techniques, and cooperative problem-solving. People can lessen the mental strain of overthinking by developing a network of support through the development of these interpersonal skills.

The Importance of Social Support

Since humans are social creatures by nature, other people's support is essential to mental health. This chapter's portion explores the value of social support in overcoming overthinking and overcoming obstacles in life.

The various types of social support—such as informational, practical, and emotional support—will be discussed by readers. The chapter sheds light on how social relationships are reciprocal and emphasizes how helping others can improve one's own wellbeing.

Active listening, empathy, and reciprocity are highlighted as helpful strategies for establishing and preserving social bonds. People who have deep relationships with others establish a safety net that lessens the isolating consequences of overthinking.

Effective Communication Skills

Healthy relationships are built on effective communication, which is also a crucial skill in minimizing the misunderstandings and misinterpretations that frequently lead to overthinking. The fundamentals of good communication, such as assertiveness, active listening, and nonverbal clues, are covered in this section.

The chapter examines typical communication errors including mind-reading, assumptions, and ambiguity that can lead to overthinking. The techniques covered in this section will help readers communicate effectively, ask for understanding from others, and resolve problems in a positive way.

People can cultivate harmonious relationships that offer a helpful framework for overcoming overthinking and improving mental well-being by developing their communication abilities.

Collaborative Problem-Solving

A collaborative approach to problem-solving that leverages the abilities and viewpoints of numerous people is called shared problem-solving. This chapter's portion examines how group problem-solving can lessen the cognitive load associated with overthinking.

The skills that readers will acquire for tackling problems as a group include open communication, brainstorming, and utilizing a variety of viewpoints. Case studies show how creative solutions and a sense of accomplishment may result from cooperative problem-solving.

The chapter highlights the value of trust and vulnerability in cooperative problem-solving, fostering an atmosphere where people feel at ease disclosing their ideas and opinions. Through utilizing the group's collective intelligence, people can release the tension caused by overanalyzing situations and maximize the efficiency of teamwork.

In summary, interacting with people is a powerful tactic for getting past overthinking. Through acknowledging the value of social support, developing proficient communication abilities, and adopting cooperative problem-solving techniques, people can establish a network of relationships that promotes adaptability, comprehension, and mutual development. The mental strain of overthinking lessens as interpersonal ties grow, opening the door to a life that is more connected and supportive.

CHAPTER 12

Mastering the Art of Focus

Learning to focus is an essential ability in the fight against overthinking and brain training. This chapter looks at methods for sharpening focus, reducing outside distractions, and teaching the brain to be in the moment. People can improve their general cognitive capacities and lessen the mental clutter that frequently results from overthinking by developing a focused mind.

Techniques for Improving Concentration

The cornerstone of efficient thought and problem-solving is concentration. This chapter's part on practical methods for enhancing attention provides readers with doable approaches to narrow their focus.

In order to teach the mind to be present, readers will examine mindfulness techniques like focused breathing and meditation. The idea of attentional control, which teaches people to consciously focus their attention and resist giving in to daydreaming, is also covered in this chapter.

The Pomodoro Technique is presented as a useful tool for improving concentration. It is a time management technique that involves focused work intervals. People can improve their concentration skills and lessen their tendency to overthink by adopting these strategies into their regular routines.

Minimizing Distractions

Distractions are everywhere in this era of continuous connectedness, and they can seriously impair focus. This section walks readers through techniques for reducing distractions in both digital and real-world settings.

In order to reduce interruptions, the chapter discusses the significance of designating specific workplaces and establishing boundaries. There includes discussion of useful strategies for controlling digital distractions, like using productivity apps and setting up dedicated work periods.

Additionally, readers will master the skill of single-tasking, which is concentrating on one activity at a time as opposed to trying to juggle several obligations. People can clear their minds and lessen the cognitive burden that leads to overthinking by reducing distractions and establishing a setting that is conducive to focus.

Training Your Brain to Stay Present

Overthinking thrives in a wandering mind, and learning to live in the present moment is a potent remedy. The chapter's exploration of mindfulness practices and cognitive approaches to developing present-moment awareness takes place in this part.

In order to promote a more focused and present-minded mindset, readers will learn the fundamentals of mindfulness meditation and how to incorporate it into everyday activities. Additionally covered in this chapter are cognitive-behavioral methods for dealing with rumination and diverting attention from unhelpful, recurring ideas.

To achieve optimal focus, the idea of flow—a state of total absorption in an activity—is introduced. People can overcome the limitations of overthinking and discover the richness of every moment by regularly practicing methods for staying present.

To sum up, developing the skill of attention is a crucial first step in teaching the brain to stop overanalyzing. People can develop a more resilient and concentrated mindset by putting strategies for enhancing focus, reducing distractions, and teaching the brain to remain in the present moment into practice. Concentration becomes stronger and the grasp of overthinking becomes less, enabling a more purposeful and fruitful interaction with the present.

CHAPTER 13

Mind-Body Connection

Gaining an understanding of the complex relationship between the body and mind is crucial to overcoming overthinking. This chapter delves into the mind-body link by examining the benefits of mindful eating, physical activity for mental clarity, and the critical function sleep plays in controlling overthinking.

Incorporating Physical Activity for Mental Clarity

Engaging in physical activity is an effective way to improve brain clarity and lessen the mental haze brought on by overthinking. This part explores the psychological and physiological effects of exercise, giving readers a thorough grasp of the relationship between the mind and body.

Readers will investigate a range of physical activities, including mindful movement techniques like yoga and tai chi and cardiovascular workouts that increase neurotransmitters. The chapter places a strong emphasis on the benefits of regular exercise for enhancing general wellbeing and on how it directly lowers stress and anxiety, two factors that frequently lead to overthinking.

There is a discussion of useful strategies for integrating physical exercise into everyday routines so that people can take advantage of the mind-body link to improve resilience and mental clarity.

Mindful Eating and its Impact

Our mental states are significantly shaped by the stuff we eat. The idea of mindful eating is examined in this section along with how it affects the mind-body relationship. The ability to eat mindfully and with intention will teach readers how to develop a healthy relationship with food that promotes mental health.

The chapter explores the significance of choosing nutritional foods that enhance cognitive function, paying attention to hunger and fullness cues, and relishing every bite. Individuals can lessen emotional eating, which is a common reaction to stress and overthinking, by developing mindful eating practices.

There is discussion of doable methods for bringing mindfulness to mealtimes, like slowing down and appreciating flavors. Through the cultivation of a positive relationship with food, people can utilize the mind-body link to enhance their general well-being and mental clarity.

The Role of Sleep in Overcoming Overthinking

It is impossible to overestimate the importance of sleep for mental health and how it affects overthinking. The importance of sleep for controlling overthinking and preserving cognitive function is discussed in this section.

The stages of sleep, the significance of good sleep hygiene, and the effects of sleep deprivation on mental health will all become clearer to readers. The chapter offers helpful advice for enhancing the quality of your sleep, such as setting up a regular sleep pattern, making your bedroom comfortable, and using relaxation techniques.

Examined is the connection between sleep and emotional control, emphasizing how getting enough sleep helps protect the brain from the mental strain that comes from overanalyzing. People can optimize the mind-body connection and lay the groundwork for enhanced mental resilience by making sleep a priority.

In conclusion, a comprehensive strategy for overcoming overthinking is to comprehend and nurture the mind-body link. People can establish a symbiotic relationship between their body and mind by emphasizing good sleep, eating mindfully, and engaging in physical activity for mental clarity. Overthinking loses its hold as the mind-body connection gets stronger, making room for a more resilient and balanced state of wellbeing.

CHAPTER 14

Nurturing Creativity

Being creative is a strong force that can improve our lives and be an effective means of combating overthinking. This chapter looks at how to accept divergent thinking, tap into your creativity, and use creativity as a tool for problem-solving.

Unleashing Your Creative Potential

Creativity is a wide range of actions and solutions; it is not just restricted to creative efforts. This chapter's part walks readers through the process of using their imaginations and distinctive viewpoints to reach their full creative potential.

The significance of encouraging a willingness to take risks, accepting ambiguity, and developing curiosity will all be covered for readers. People can reconnect with their inner creativity and see difficulties through a creative lens with the aid of useful exercises and prompts.

The chapter places a strong emphasis on the idea that everyone is creative and that discovering one's creative potential might offer a different approach to problem-solving and breaking the pattern of overanalyzing.

Embracing Divergent Thinking

Divergent thinking, which entails coming up with several concepts and answers, is a crucial aspect of creativity. This part explores the idea of diverse thinking and encourages readers to consider many angles and options when confronted with obstacles.

The techniques covered in this article will help readers think more creatively, including mind mapping, brainstorming, and looking for inspiration in a variety of places. The chapter promotes changing one's perspective from looking for the one "right" option to considering a variety of feasible answers.

Divergent thinking can help people overcome the limitations of overthinking, creating fresh opportunities for original problem-solving and decision-making.

Using Creativity to Solve Problems

Being creative is more than simply a frivolous endeavor; it's an effective means of solving problems. This chapter's part examines how using imagination might help you take on obstacles and get past the mental barriers that come with overthinking.

By using divergent thinking to come up with a variety of possible answers, readers will learn to see difficulties as opportunities for creative discovery. The chapter illustrates the adaptability of a creative mentality by offering instances of creative problem-solving across a range of industries.

Readers are guided through the process of applying creativity to specific difficulties they may be facing through practical exercises. Through the acquisition of creative problem-solving techniques, individuals might develop a proactive and inventive strategy for surmounting overthinking.

To sum up, fostering creativity is a game-changing tactic in the fight against overthinking. People may add innovation and resilience to their lives by embracing divergent thinking, utilizing creativity as a problem-solving tool, and unleashing their creative potential. The hold of overthinking weakens as the creative mentality takes hold, opening the door to a more dynamic and innovative response to life's obstacles.

CHAPTER 15

A Mindful and Productive Future

Now that this journey to overcome overthinking is coming to an end, let's take a moment to evaluate what we've learned, acknowledge our accomplishments, and set off on a path toward a more thoughtful and productive future. This last chapter sums up the trip in its whole and provides advice on reflecting, maintaining good changes, and confidently continuing forward.

Reflecting on the Journey

Pause to consider the journey you've taken to get rid of your overthinking. Recognize the obstacles encountered, the tactics used, and the personal development gained during the process. Think back on the realizations you had from each chapter and how they helped you modify your daily routine and perspective.

When you look back on the experience, you have the chance to honor the fortitude, commitment, and bravery that propelled your endeavors. It's an opportunity to recognize your growth and your enhanced comprehension of your own mental terrain. Accept this reflective moment with a feeling of success and thankfulness for the knowledge gained.

72

Sustaining Positive Changes

A more conscientious and productive future is illuminated by positive transformation. The significance of maintaining the constructive changes started during the journey is examined in this portion of the conclusion. Determine which routines, approaches, and mental modifications have worked best to prevent overthinking.

Make a strategy for regularly implementing these constructive adjustments into your everyday routine. Make a commitment to include these components in your daily routine, whether it's the development of healthy habits, the embrace of creativity, or the practice of mindfulness. Maintaining positive improvements strengthens your resilience against the recurrence of overthinking. Consistency is the key to long-lasting change.

Moving Forward with Confidence

Now that you have a toolset of methods and fresh ideas, it's time to confidently face the future. You are encouraged to picture the kind of person you want to be and the kind of life you want to lead in this part. Establish attainable, empowering goals that support your general wellbeing and are consistent with your values.

Accept the self-assurance that results from overcoming overthinking's obstacles. Acknowledge that obstacles are a part of the process and that every moment is a chance for improvement. You regain control over your thoughts and behaviors when you move forward with confidence, which opens the door to a more aware and fruitful life.

In summary, the road to overcoming overthinking is a dynamic process of self-discovery and development rather than a straight line. As you consider the lessons you've learned, maintain the progress you've made, and confidently go forward, never forget that this transition is a continuous process. Accept the trip with curiosity and openness, knowing that every step will lead to a future that is more resilient, conscious, and fruitful.

We appreciate you starting this path of introspection and development. I hope you have a clear sense of purpose, delight in the present, and a bright future.